Memory Art

Memory Art

30 ideas for shadowboxes and other keepsake displays

Mary Lynn Maloney

Printed in the United States of America

11 10 09 08 07   1 2 3 4 5

Publisher's Cataloging-in-Publication Data *(Prepared by The Donohue Group, Inc.)*
Maloney, Mary Lynn.
   Memory art : 30 ideas for shadowboxes and other keepsake displays / Mary Lynn Maloney.
      p. : ill. ; cm.
   ISBN: 978-0-87116-251-9
1. Assemblage (Art) 2. Souvenirs (Keepsakes) 3. Box making. 4. Ornamental boxes. 4. I. Title.
TT910 .M34 2007
749.7

Foreword

My husband, Victor, and I took a glorious, perspective-changing trip around the world back in the late '90s. We spent a year backpacking and exploring different countries and cultures, and along the way, we accumulated several boxes worth of memorabilia. When we got settled back in the States, I incorporated some of our travel treasures into collages, combining them with photos in a set of scrapbook albums. These books were delightful, but a lot of memorabilia remained, particularly three-dimensional souvenirs. These items sat and waited in their various boxes and bags, taking up space in the shadowy corners of our closets. After our last move, I rummaged through one of these boxes and relived lots of little moments from our trip. A receipt from a café in Slovenia, for example, made my mouth water for the pastries and fragrant coffee we savored there. I decided that I wanted these mementos to be a part of my everyday surroundings, not buried in a closet, out of sight, out of mind. I began pulling out bits and pieces from our travels and using them as elements in three-dimensional memory art to display in our home. These "travel features," as Victor calls them, always draw viewers in for a closer study of the intriguing objects within the composition.

This book is intended to inspire those of you who have been saving boxes and bags of your photos, mementos, and three-dimensional souvenirs for "someday." I hope to give you a gentle nudge toward making that someday happen, sooner rather than later. In these pages, you will find many ideas to help you create meaningful and one-of-a-kind memory art that encapsulates special moments in your life. You will find project ideas for creating artistic displays using your unique collections as focal points. You will see how to incorporate keepsakes into pieces that celebrate holidays and life's milestones. And you will find projects that illustrate ways to honor your heritage, or memorialize friends, relatives, and pets. All the projects are designed to show you how fun it can be to get your mementos out of those boxes and into your artwork.

My very best wishes to you in your creative endeavors. Have a great time turning your cherished memories into beautiful art.

Mary Lynn

Contents

Dedication

To Victor, who encourages my creativity, makes me laugh, acts as my shipping clerk, and mixes a mean martini.

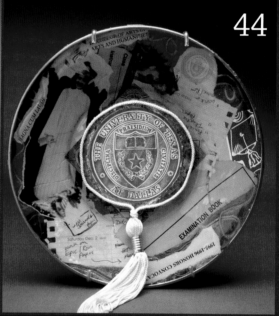

60

Getting Started

Priceless collectibles and family heirlooms

I designed the projects in this book to incorporate keepsakes that have more sentimental value than monetary value. If you own a pair of Queen Victoria's opera glasses, you probably don't want to glue them into a shadowbox collage. A valuable item like that should be preserved, stored, and displayed with the help of a professional archivist. But you can get creative about incorporating the opera glasses into your art: Take a close-up photo of the opera glasses, print it on watercolor paper in a sepia tone, and frame the photo in an ornate Victorian-style frame. Use that as the focal point in your memory art and save the real glasses for the historians.

This brings me to a very important point: Please make sure you have the authority to use whatever memento you have in mind. If you want to use Grandma's vintage doily and apply an iron-on photo transfer, make sure you are the one who can make that decision. It's not right to pinch a doily that belongs to your cousin Rita (no matter how bossy she is) and alter it with inks, paints, or glues. If Mom has left you her wedding dress, you are free to use some of the lace as an element in your art. Some people are uncomfortable with this concept, but consider this: If no granddaughter is interested in wearing Mom's wedding dress, and it is destined to languish, unseen and unappreciated, in a storage box, wouldn't it be a better way to honor her memory by using a piece of the dress in an elegant and stylish piece of memory art?

Many of the items I have used in these projects are my own, one-of-a-kind, personal keepsakes, so your finished project, of course, will look different. But that's what is so wonderful about creating memory art; yours is unique and reflects your experiences. If you absolutely fall in love with a keepsake I've used, such as a vintage crocheted Santa, it's likely you can find a similar item in an antique shop, at a flea market, or on eBay. While the keepsakes are the stars of the artwork, all of the supporting characters, such as art supplies, shadowboxes, papers, beads, rubber stamps, and embellishments, are available at art and craft stores.

I supply written instructions on how to create the specific projects shown. This gives you the opportunity to apply a particular technique, achieve the same color, or create the same background texture that I have. I've given measurements pertinent to each project, but if you use a canvas that is square where mine is rectangular, you will obviously need to make adjustments. Consider the instructions guidelines, supplying the technical information you need while allowing you plenty of creative room to develop your unique version of the project.

archival issues

Do your best to follow sensible archival guidelines when creating memory art. Make prints of photographs, particularly rare or vintage photos, and use the prints in your artwork. Store the originals in acid-free envelopes and archival-quality photo boxes. When a photocopy is used in an art piece, make the copy on a laser printer or toner-based copier. Ink-jet copies can fade very quickly. Photocopies can be treated with a product such as Krylon's Preserve-It, an acid-free spray that helps protect and prolong the life of photos and printed papers. Keep photos and paper ephemera away from cellophane tape, cardboard, or anything that has high acidity.

Layer photos on acid-free cardstocks or mats.

To protect your finished artwork from the fading caused by UV rays, hang or display it away from direct sunlight. I like to see and feel the texture of my finished pieces, so I don't often cover my work with glass. I make a point of dusting these "open" pieces to help protect them and keep them looking fresh. When I do use glass, I choose a UV-protectant variety or a piece of acrylic, which also helps protect against UV damage. For much more in-depth information on framing and preservation, visit a local frame shop and speak with a professional.

The main objective in making

memory art is to create work that reflects your connections with family and friends. The artwork is meant to be enjoyed and to bring pleasure to you or the recipient. Follow common-sense archival practices, but don't fret that your art might not last 500 years. Enjoy the creative process.

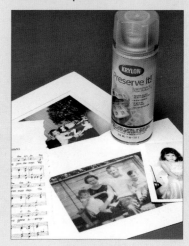

Foundations

Ready-made shadowboxes are available in a variety of sizes at art and craft stores or online. Although these handy boxes are a great starting point, consider other creative alternatives for a foundation as you move forward with your art. Canvases, crates, old drawers, metal grates, jewelry boxes, plates, cigar boxes, and lunch boxes are just a few alternate surfaces to explore.

The focus or theme of your memory art can guide you in choosing a foundation. If you want to commemorate a writer friend for a career achievement, for example, consider using the cover of an old, beat-up dictionary as the base of your artwork. I am a firm believer in recycling, and I find many of my art surfaces at garage sales and flea markets. Goodwill or Habitat for Humanity stores are fabulous sources for materials, plus your purchases help support hardworking and compassionate enterprises. I often find discarded paintings in very nice frames at these thrift stores. The price is right, and it's easy to transform them with some sandpaper, gesso, and paint.

Sometimes I come across a shadowbox that is just the right size for what I have in mind, but I want to customize it a little. A simple way to add some impact is to add a frame. Shadowboxes and frames are made in very similar sizes, so attaching a frame to a shadowbox takes just a few steps.

How to attach a frame to a shadowbox

1 Squeeze wood glue around rim of shadowbox.

2 Lay frame on top and clamp to shadowbox.

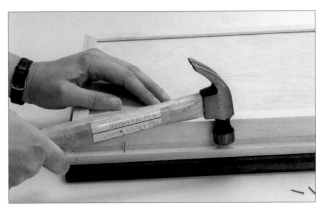

3 For added structural security, nail the pieces together all around. The framed shadowbox is now ready for painting or any artistic treatment.

Now that you have a foundation for your memory art, take the time to add a nice, sturdy hanger on the back. Don't make the mistake I did and create a really cool piece of art within a box, then realize you have no way to hang it. I ended up crushing a few objects in and on the box when I turned the piece over to attach the hardware for my hanger!

Dragon's teeth hangers or simple wire loops will work for lightweight pieces of memory art. For heavier pieces, it is worth taking the time to attach picture-hanging wire to the back.

How to attach picture-hanging wire

Position D-ring hanging hardware about one-third of the way down and attach with screws. Loop hanging wire through D-rings and twist ends to secure. Snip excess with wire cutters. Attach felt pads or museum putty to bottom corners. Your hanger is attached, and now you can get creative!

Choosing adhesives

Choosing glues for your memory art projects can be confusing – even overwhelming – because there are so many kinds available. Different properties of different materials require different formulas to make them adhere. Here is some basic information that I hope will help get you off to a good start. The list is not exhaustive by any means; it merely includes products I use or am familiar with. The brand listed first in each category is the product used in the projects in this book, and is what I recommend when I teach memory art techniques. Feel free to try others or stick with your favorites.

I want to glue...	Example	Glue type(s)	Common brand names
nonporous material to a porous surface	charm, button, or rhinestone to paper, fabric, wood, or canvas	generally referred to as **tacky glues**	**Beacon Adhesives Gem-Tac** Aleene's Jewel-It Crafter's Pick Jewel Bond Elmer's Craft Bond
porous material to a porous surface	paper to paper	**glue sticks, spray adhesives, sticky glue dots, tapes, adhesive machines, light-body craft glues**	**Beacon Adhesives Paper-Tac** Aleene's Original Tacky Glue Elmer's Glue-All GlueDots Krylon Spray Adhesive UHU USArtQuest Perfect Paper Adhesive
	fabric to fabric (or other material)	**fabric glues** • formulated to not seep through • washable or dry-cleanable • flexible, not brittle, when dry	**Beacon Adhesives Fabri-Tac** Crafters Pick Fabric Glue
	Styrofoam	**specialty glue** made just for Styrofoam	StyroGlue
nonporous material to a nonporous surface	charms, mosaic tiles, or beads to glass, metal, or plastic	often called **permanent glues**	**Beacon Adhesives Glass, Metal & More** Aleene's Platinum Bond 7800 Crafter's Pick The Ultimate!
		glues designed to **grab and hold quickly**	**Beacon Adhesives Quick Grip** Aleene's Quick-Dry Tacky Glue Super Glue
		glues with **fine-point nozzles** to help with precision work such as jewelry	**Beacon Adhesives Dazzle-Tac** GS Hypo Cement

Collage and decoupage adhesive

I do a lot of collage art, and have shown and sold my work for the past several years at art fairs and galleries. My absolute favorite adhesive to use for collage is gel medium. Gel medium is a paste-like product that is a basic acrylic emulsion. It is used with acrylic paints to create glazes or change the thickness of a paint. But it is also a great adhesive. It can be easily brushed on, just like paint.

Over the years, I've found that gel medium is very effective for adhering everything from tissue paper to corrugated cardboard to medium-weight metallic objects onto my collage pieces. For lighter-weight items, I dilute the gel with a little water and use it just like a decoupage medium. The heavier-weight items require a heavyweight medium.

the art of collage

Initial attempt

Stronger composition

Making choices about what items to include in your composition and how to arrange them falls into the realm of collage (one of my favorite places). Consider how elements relate to each other and how a viewer's eye will be invited in and shown around your work. The two shadowbox collages above illustrate my point. They were constructed in the same frame and use the same elements (travel keepsakes and a piece of gold trim).

The first sample is OK. It represents many people's initial attempts at collage. The piece holds an interesting assortment of travel memorabilia; the coins are intriguing and add some nice dimension. A viewer might step up to take a closer look but may not linger. Overall, the piece is a bit lackluster; it has the look of a bulletin board, where lots of things have been pinned on, and images and colors just blend together. Everything is included, but nothing is very important. The composition just doesn't engage the eye.

The second sample is a stronger composition overall. Why? The memorabilia are arranged in layers that achieve more depth. Related items, such as the tickets and the postage stamps, are grouped close

to make a stronger statement. The gold trim has become part of the composition and serves as a line that bridges different items, making them relate and connect with one another. The visually heavy photo at the top right is now counterbalanced with the heavyweight coins in the lower left. I have added one element: I inked the edges of the tickets. This creates contrast and allows the tickets to "pop" instead of simply blending into the background. The photo shows a village where buildings overlook the sea in a delightfully staggered fashion. Stacking and staggering the postage stamps and tickets is a way to mimic the stacked rooftops of the village. This piece has a tighter, more cohesive feeling, and a viewer's eye would be pleased to travel around here for a while.

As you experiment with arranging your memory art, you will become more and more intuitive about placing something here, rather than there. At first, you might say to yourself, "I'm putting this ribbon here to connect these two unrelated things." But after a while, you will just do it without a conscious thought about why. Your eye, and heart, and soul know why. Eventually they'll take the driver's seat.

TIP

Use low-tack tape to hold items in place as you consider their arrangement.

4 Thread spools onto dowel rods and play with color and size variations **[D]**. Glue a few random spool tops and bottoms together with quick-gripping permanent glue. Arrange assembled thread columns and photo doily in drawer. Glue thread columns to top and bottom of drawer with quick-grip glue. Glue photo doily to top, back, and side of drawer with dots of fabric glue.

5 Dot fabric glue to to sweater backgr more random pins to adhere remaining kee Use fabric glue to adh bottom edges of draw

llinery Memories

great collection of vintage millinery trims, some of which came
s belonging to my grandmother. I also have a photo of her
my great-grandmother) wearing a gorgeous hat that dates
turn of the 19th century. All these hat-related items are finally
together in – what else? – the lid of a hatbox.

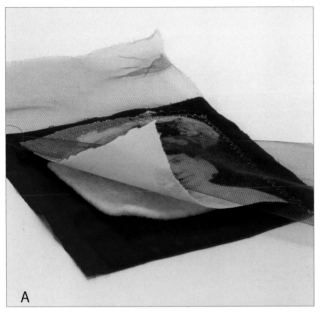

A

B

materials

- hatbox lid, 11 in. (28cm) diam.
- personal keepsake items: millinery trims (spool of gray velvet piping, fabric leaves, feathers, wired pearls), hat pins, buttons, photocopy
- 2 yd. (1.8m) ea. tulle: white, purple
- 1 yd. (.9m) narrow braid, maroon
- 1 yd. wide grosgrain ribbon, teal
- 1 yd. jacquard ribbon, pink
- 7 in. (18cm) square of velvet, red
- 4 in. (10cm) square of batting, ⅛-in. (3mm) thick
- matte-finish spray sealer
- sewing machine
- sewing threads: pink, white, teal, purple
- round initial sticker
- oval jewelry finding
- fabric glue
- tacky glue
- scissors

1 Apply fabric glue lightly to inside bottom of hatbox. Press approximately half of purple tulle gently into hatbox, creating soft folds and gathers. Tie random knots in a yard of velvet piping and adhere over tulle, around inner perimeter of box lid. Glue wide teal ribbon horizontally across inner box lid. Fold ends around to back, glue, and trim excess ribbon. Repeat with pink jacquard ribbon, gluing it over teal ribbon. Cut 10 in. (25cm) of velvet piping, knot the ends, and glue onto pink ribbon.

2 Tear photocopy to 5 in. (13cm) square. Make a sandwich of red velvet square, batting, and torn photo. Cut a piece of purple tulle to approximately 6 x 12 in. (15 x 30cm). Lay on top of sandwich **[A]**. Pin all layers together. Thread machine with pink thread on top and white thread in bobbin. Stitch sandwich together using a wide zig-zag stitch.

3 Hand-sew five buttons to left side of assembled photo sandwich (use teal and purple threads). Use fabric glue to adhere photo sandwich to center of box lid. Glue one button to lower right corner. Push two hat pins through upper right area of photo sandwich. Glue a large button on top of crossed hat pins. Glue initial sticker to top of large button. (My great-grandmother's name was Katherine, so I used the letter K.)

4 Glue half of white tulle around outer perimeter of box lid. Gather millinery feathers, fabric leaves, and pearl trim, glue together at bottom, and wrap with a yard each of velvet piping, maroon braid, and white tulle. Glue assembled hat trims over bottom left edge of photo, letting long ends dangle over side of box lid. Trim to desired length and knot ends of piping and braids.

5 Create an easy hanger on the back using a length of grosgrain ribbon looped through an oval jewelry finding. Adhere with a generous amount of fabric glue and let dry thoroughly before hanging **[B]**.

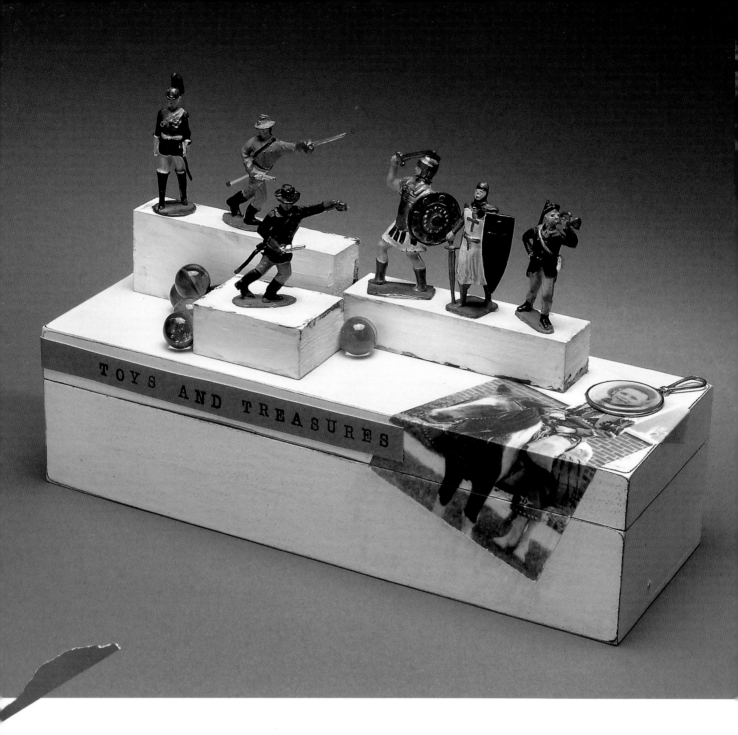

Toys & Treasures
Collection Box

Every little boy seems to have a motley collection of treasures: game pieces, miniature cars, toy soldiers, dirt clods, string. It might seem like an odd assortment, but this collection actually holds great display potential.

materials

- wood box with hinged lid, 11 x 3 x 4 in. (28 x 8 x 10cm)
- solid wood whittler's kit
- personal keepsake items: photocopy of childhood photo, tin soldiers, marbles, toy magnifying glass
- acrylic paints: raw umber, vanilla
- matte-finish spray sealer
- gel medium
- cardstock, brown
- alphabet rubber stamps
- permanent ink, black
- quick-gripping permanent glue
- fast-drying paper glue
- medium-grit sandpaper
- clean, lint-free rag
- paintbrush
- craft knife with new blade
- scissors

1 Sand any rough areas on box and wipe clean. Paint box with a coat of raw umber and let dry.

2 Paint over raw umber with a light coat of vanilla [A]. Let dry.

3 Give box an aged look by sanding vanilla paint from edges, corners, and random areas of box to expose dark color underneath [B]. Wipe clean with rag.

4 Spray photocopy with matte spray to seal. Using gel medium, decoupage photocopy to right edge of box top and front. Let dry. Slice photo along seam with craft knife so box will open.

5 Repeat painting and sanding process from steps 1 and 2 on three different sizes of wood blocks from whittler's kit. Let dry. Use quick-gripping permanent glue to adhere blocks to wooden box top. Let dry.

6 Glue assorted toy soldiers and marbles on and around wood blocks. Glue magnifying glass over photo.

7 Use alphabet stamps and black ink to spell out "toys and treasures" onto brown cardstock. Cut cardstock into narrow strip and use fast-drying paper glue to adhere onto front and left edge of box lid.

PB&J Artwork Display

A lunch box and children's drawings – two delightful representatives of childhood – come together in this whimsical keepsake display.

1 Open lunch box and lay flat on work surface. Crop selected children's photos and drawings to desired sizes. Move items around on face of lunch box until you are pleased with the arrangement. Glue photos and drawings to box.

2 Glue puffy heart trim across top of lunch box and along select photo(s). Squeeze a very thin line of glue around select portions of photos and drawings. Press red yarn onto line of glue. Work slowly, gluing a small portion at a time. Step back every now and then to see if you like how the yarn outline looks.

3 Create random yarn spirals by gluing a small circle shape and coiling yarn onto circle. Gather 8-10 pieces of yarn together and cut to approximately 6 in. (15cm). Tie yarn into a knot and trim top and bottom. Repeat process, creating a second yarn tassel. Glue tassels to right and left bottom corners of lunch box.

materials

- personal keepsake items: old metal lunch box, children's drawing, photos
- 1 yd. (.9m) puffy heart trim
- $1/2$ yd. (46cm) grosgrain ribbon, black and white
- skein of yarn, dark red
- fast-drying paper glue
- scissors

TIP This playful piece can be displayed several ways: Open the box, letting the hinged lid fall downward, and hang it from two small nails. It looks charming on a kitchen wall. Or, close the box and use it in a playroom to store crayons or art supplies.

Changeable Art Gallery

A special gallery board with the sole purpose of displaying a child's artwork makes the artist feel special as well. The magnetic surface enables you to change the work so a new piece can be featured every week.

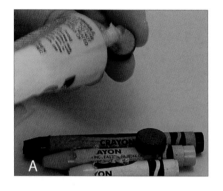

A

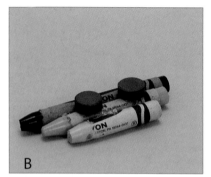

B

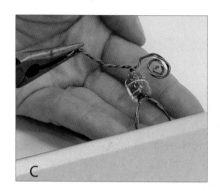

C

1 Wash and dry cookie sheet. Apply 3-4 coats of burgundy spray paint.

2 Spell out "art" with dimensional letters and glue to top center of cookie sheet. Glue a crayon on either side of word. Repeat with bottom of cookie tray, spelling out "gallery."

3 Using crayon sharpener, trim a crayon to 1¾ in. (4.4cm), another to 2½ in. (6.4cm), and a third to 3 in. (7.6cm). Glue crayons together, creating a triangular shape **[A]**. Repeat, creating three more crayon bundles. Let dry thoroughly. Glue two magnets to the back of each crayon bundle **[B]**.

4 To create a hanging hook, loop plastic-coated wire through tubular opening on back of cookie sheet. Twist wire into a large circular loop. Slide red bead over top. Slide spacer bead next to red bead. Twist to secure beads. Use jewelry pliers to coil ends of twisted wire **[C]**.

TIP Make sure you use or purchase a metal cookie sheet! Take a magnet with you to the store and test a few cookie sheets. Aluminum won't work.

materials

- metal cookie sheet, 12 x 19 in. (30 x 48cm)
- latex spray paint, burgundy
- 8 round magnets
- 16 crayons, various colors
- crayon sharpener
- dimensional alphabet stickers, ⅝ in. (1.6cm)
- ½ yd. (46cm) plastic-coated craft wire
- large-hole glass bead, red
- silver spacer bead
- jewelry pliers
- quick-gripping permanent glue

TIP A dot of museum putty on each bottom back corner of the cookie sheet will help keep the sheet steady against the wall.

Coin of the Realm Shadowbox

Lots of people save coins from their travels, only to stick them in a bag or box. Why not select some favorite shapes and sizes and incorporate them into a shadowbox? The coins' metallic shine will add a lovely, rich patina to your finished piece.

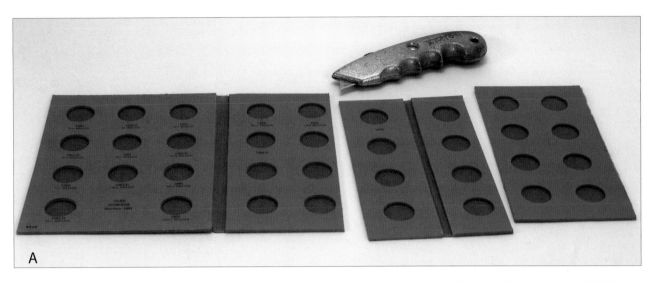

A

1 Paint wood shadowbox overall with two coats black paint, letting it dry between applications.

2 Enlarge photo to about 6 x 8 in. (15 x 20cm). Copy in black and white onto ivory cardstock. Trim photo and use glue stick to adhere it to left-hand side of shadowbox. Use fabric glue to adhere a length of velvet ribbon across top edge of shadowbox.

3 Adhere travel stickers to upper right and lower left corners of shadowbox. Lightly tap and rub Distress Ink directly from pad onto stickers, giving them an aged appearance.

4 Use box-cutter knife to cut a hinged section from coin-collection folder [A].

5 Use fabric glue to adhere a length of velvet ribbon down center of coin slots. Use quick-grip glue to adhere selected coins over ribbon [B]. Glue assembled coin folder onto right side of shadowbox, angling it downward to rest on edge of photo.

6 Glue additional coins across top of shadowbox and over excess velvet ribbon on lower right side of shadowbox.

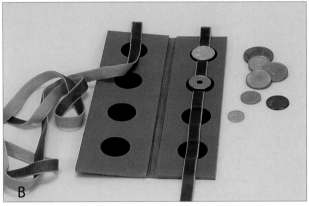

B

materials

- personal keepsake items: foreign coins, travel photo, old coin-collection folder
- square wood shadowbox, 10¼ in. (26cm)
- acrylic paint, black
- photocopier
- ivory cardstock
- 5 travel poster stickers
- Tim Holtz Distress Ink, Vintage Photo
- 2 yd. (1.8m) narrow velvet ribbon, brown
- glue stick
- fabric glue
- quick-gripping permanent glue
- scissors
- box-cutter knife

Travel Keepsake Tower

This art piece is practical as well as beautiful. Stack the hatboxes and display them with framed travel photos or a stack of travel albums. Use the boxes to store foreign currency, postcards, tickets, and other travel memorabilia.

1 Crush brown kraft paper into a ball, then flatten out. Cover hatboxes with paper, using fast-drying paper glue to adhere. Fold excess paper onto inside and bottom of box. Trim excess. Rub surface of paper with light brown ink (directly from inkpad). Let dry. Randomly stamp compass in red ink around boxes.

2 Glue assorted paper currency around boxes. Follow rub-on package instructions and rub several sayings onto covered boxes. Adhere word stickers onto boxes.

3 Spray paint box lids with suede paint. Apply 2-3 coats for even coverage. Let dry. Glue ribbons around edges of box lids. Cut 14 in. (36cm) of ribbon and tie knots a few inches from both ends. Glue knots to sides of small box lid, creating a faux handle. Glue a saying across ribbon handle.

materials

- personal keepsake items: foreign paper currency
- hatbox, 8-in. (20cm) diam.
- hatbox, 9-in. (23cm) diam.
- kraft paper, brown
- permanent dye inkpads: light brown, red
- suede-textured spray paint, sienna
- 3 yd. (2.7m) stripe grosgrain ribbon
- compass rubber stamp
- themed rub-ons and word stickers
- fast-drying paper glue
- fabric glue
- scissors

Old World Memory Map

Dress up a dull corkboard and make it a canvas for displaying travel photos and souvenirs. The custom-made pushpins hold images of places you've been, or places you dream of visiting.

A

materials

- framed corkboard, 22 x 17 in. (56 x 43cm)
- personal keepsake items: travel photos, postcards, tickets
- Old World map reproduction
- acrylic texturizing medium
- acrylic paints: dark green, asphalt
- matte gel medium
- 5 flat glass pebbles, assorted tints
- 5 pushpins
- quick-gripping permanent glue
- soft cotton rag
- paintbrush

1 Mix equal amounts texturizing medium and dark green acrylic paint. Brush onto wooden frame of corkboard. Let dry. Mix a few drops of asphalt acrylic with 2-3 teaspoons of water. Brush randomly over dark green. Let dry a few minutes, then wipe off random areas with a rag.

2 Tear edges of map to fit within corkboard. Thin gel medium with a little water and brush onto surface of corkboard. Lay map onto corkboard. Brush gel medium over map. Smooth out any wrinkles. Let dry.

3 Lay a glass pebble over an interesting area of printed travel memorabilia. Trace around pebble and cut out circle of paper **[A]**. Brush bottom of pebble with gel medium. Glue paper circle, right side up, onto pebble bottom. Brush back of paper with gel medium. Repeat process with remaining pebbles. Let dry.

4 Use quick-gripping permanent glue to adhere heads of pushpins to bottoms of pebbles **[B]**. Let dry. Pin selected travel photos and mementos to corkboard.

B

TIP I recycled a thrift store corkboard for this project, and the poster featuring an Old World map was an eBay find.

Joyful Season Card Display

Here is a nice way to combine old and new. Christmas cards saved from years past make up the mosaic background, while the hanging streamers display the cards you receive during the current holiday season. Bring out this piece each year and make a new tradition of displaying cards in a uniquely elegant fashion.

A

B

1 Create a wash with equal parts dark green paint and water. Paint wooden frame overall. Let dry. Randomly brush wash onto frame. Let dry. Brush metallic green paint randomly onto frame. Let dry. Use fingers to apply olive wax rub-on randomly around frame. Repeat with deep gold rub-on. Set frame aside to dry thoroughly.

2 Lay illustration board onto canvas. Cut canvas to the size of board plus 4 in. (10cm) all around. Adhere board to canvas. Wrap and glue canvas around to back side of board, mitering corners to reduce bulk. Cut a scrap piece of canvas and adhere to back of board, covering all raw edges. Insert canvas into frame and secure with necessary hardware on back.

3 Cut old Christmas cards into varied sizes of triangles and rectangles **[A]**. Glue shapes onto board, leaving a narrow margin of canvas between shapes **[B]**. Cut pieces as needed to fit together, much like doing a puzzle. Continue until entire board is covered in a paper mosaic.

4 Paint papier mâché letters overall with several coats of metallic green. Let dry. Apply eggplant ink directly from pad onto edges of papier mâché letters. Let dry. Glue letters to paper mosaic.

5 Drill three small pilot holes into bottom edge of frame. Dip ends of eye screws into a bit of glue, then screw one into each hole.

materials

- heavy illustration board, 16 x 12 in. (41 x 30cm)
- 1 yd. (.9m) canvas
- wood frame (this one is a Goodwill find)
- personal keepsake items: saved Christmas cards
- 8-in. (20cm) papier mâché letters: J, O, Y
- acrylic paints: dark green, metallic green
- Mini-metallics Wax Rub-ons Kit
- pigment ink, eggplant
- 3 eye screws
- spool of ⅜-in. (1cm) velvet ribbon, sage green
- silver spiral clips
- tacky glue
- craft drill with ¹⁄₁₆-in. (2mm) bit
- scissors
- paintbrush

6 Cut three lengths of sage green velvet ribbon, varying lengths from 38 to 45 in. (96-114cm). Thread a ribbon through an eye screw and glue end of ribbon to itself to secure. Repeat with remaining ribbons. Slide spiral clips onto ribbons as needed to hold selected Christmas cards.

Keepsake

a new addition or celebrate a little one's first
...heerful keepsake.

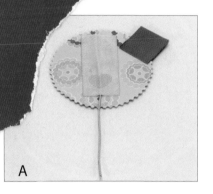

A

B

...er to the consistency of
...ximately ¼ teaspoon Spring
...arlwhite pigment powders.
...ps water. Tear mulberry paper
...gel medium mixture to decoup-
...m disk. Be sure to brush mixture over
...er disk completely. Let dry.

...glue to adhere three woven labels to front
...foam disk. Glue mini ball fringe around disk,
...outer edge.

...ut baby photo into a 2-in. (5cm) circle. Adhere
...to cardstock with glue stick. Trim cardstock with
decorative-edge scissors, leaving a narrow frame around
photo. Glue a woven label to upper left of assembled
photo. Cut 4 in. (10cm) of wire and center it on back of
assembled photo. Glue a long, narrow woven label over
wire to secure it to photo back **[A]**.

4 Drill a hole through center of cork. Dab a little quick-
gripping permanent glue on end of wire and push
wire through cork. Create a small coil on end of cork
using jewelry pliers **[B]**.

5 Loop and tie 4-6 fibers onto wire coil. Secure fibers to
coil with a dab of fabric glue. Cut fibers to hang about
5 in. (13cm) from end of coil. Thread beads and charms
randomly onto fibers, securing with knots. Trim fibers
to varying lengths. Drop beaded fibers into baby bottle
and push cork into mouth of bottle. Use quick-grip glue
to adhere assembled bottle onto center back area of
decorated foam disk.

6 Tie laces of baby shoes into secure bows. Thread two
woven labels onto ends of shoelaces. Secure with a
dab of fabric glue behind each label. Use quick-grip glue
to adhere baby shoes to foam disk.

materials

- craft foam disk, 7-in. (18cm) diam.
- personal keepsake items:
  photo, vintage baby bottle,
  baby shoes, baby-themed
  charms
- mulberry paper, pale green
- matte gel medium
- Pearl Ex Pigments: Spring
  Green, Pearlwhite

- baby-themed woven labels
- mini ball fringe, light green
- patterned cardstock,
  bright green
- craft cork
- 16-gauge wire
- pastel fashion fibers
- 3-5 assorted glass beads,
  greens and blues

- glue stick
- quick-gripping permanent glue
- fabric glue
- scissors
- craft drill with ¹⁄₁₆-in. (2mm) bit
- paintbrush
- decorative-edge scissors
- flatnose jewelry pliers
- wire cutters

Happy Grad
Keepsake Plate

After years of hard work and the solemnity of a graduation ceremony, it's time to kick up your heels and celebrate! Festive papers and gold leaf combine with fragments of paper memorabilia to create a joyful piece of art.

A

materials

- glass plate, 8-in. (20cm) diam.
- personal keepsake items: graduation program, photos, and cards; academic calendar notes; class papers; tassel
- Perfect Paper Adhesive, matte
- Duo Embellishing Adhesive
- Gildenglitz Variegated gilding leaf
- mulberry papers: pink, purple, green, blue
- Lumiere paint, metallic bronze
- fabric glue
- paintbrushes: bristle, foam
- craft knife
- scissors

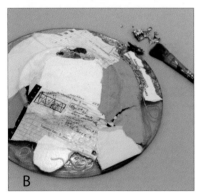

B

C

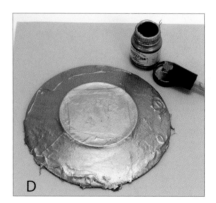

D

1 Wash and dry glass plate. Tear paper memorabilia into pieces. Pour a little Perfect Paper Adhesive (PPA) into small cup. Brush front of a paper memorabilia fragment with PPA and apply to back of glass plate. Brush back of paper with more PPA. Continue applying memorabilia to back of plate, but do not cover entire plate. Cut a few strands from tassel. Adhere to back of plate, creating random swirls **[A]**. Turn plate to right side as you work to make sure you like the placement of the pieces. Let dry.

2 Brush a light coat of Duo Embellishing Adhesive onto random clear areas on plate back, leaving some areas of glass clear for the next step. Let dry to a tacky finish. Place a bit of Gildenglitz over a tacky area and gently rub with fingers. Use a soft, dry paintbrush to brush away excess gilding leaf **[B]**. Return any scraps to package.

3 Tear mulberry papers into small pieces. Use PPA to adhere papers to any remaining clear areas on back of plate **[C]**. Brush a coat of PPA onto backs of papers to

seal. Check front of plate as you work to ensure that all clear areas get covered. Let dry.

4 Coat back of plate with bronze paint **[D]**. Let dry. Use craft knife to carefully trim away any excess paper around perimeter of plate. Paint front rim of plate with bronze and let dry.

5 Apply a ring of gilding leaf to front center circle of plate, using same process as in step 2. Tear school medallion from graduation program and glue over gold ring. Use small dabs of fabric glue to adhere tassel around medallion.

Wedding Keepsake Decor

Share some memories of your wedding in an elegant, unexpected way. This arrangement of orbs in a bowl incorporates small photos and bits of wedding memorabilia. Display the bowl alongside your wedding album, on a shelf, or atop a table.

A

materials

- shallow bamboo bowl
- personal keepsake items: wedding cards and envelopes, copies of wedding photos
- 2 craft foam balls, 14 in. (36cm)
- 3 craft foam balls, 10 in. (25cm)
- heavy-gauge craft wire
- block of scrap foam
- 1 package cocktail napkins
- assorted fabric leaves
- 5 skeleton leaves
- 1 yd. (.9m) trim, rust
- ½ yd. (46cm) braided trim
- woven wedding labels
- copper mini brads
- reindeer moss
- matte gel medium
- fabric glue
- scissors
- craft knife

1 To keep the craft foam balls steady as you work, cut pieces of heavy-gauge wire and insert into craft foam balls. Insert other end of wire into a large block of scrap foam. Tear cocktail napkins into small pieces. Thin gel medium with water (to the consistency of heavy cream), brush a little onto the ball, and adhere torn napkin pieces until ball is covered **[A]**. Brush a coat of gel medium over top of napkin pieces. Use the same decoupage process to randomly adhere fabric leaves and skeleton leaves to balls.

2 Select images or words from wedding cards and tear into small pieces. Repeat process with the envelopes that the cards came in, using torn, dated postage marks or cancelled stamps. Use decoupage process to adhere randomly to balls. Let dry.

3 Use fabric glue to adhere rust trim around small balls.

4 Tear copies of wedding photos into small rectangles or squares. Use copper brads to attach one or two photos to each large ball: Poke a small hole into a corner of a photo, then press unopened brad through the hole and into the foam. Glue a woven wedding label next to each photo. Glue pieces of braided trim next to each photo.

5 Fill bamboo bowl with reindeer moss. Arrange decorated balls on moss.

Milestone Birthday Toast

Create a special piece of art for a longtime pal who has hit a milestone birthday. This glittery and free-flowing wall hanging reflects the dynamic personality of a fun-loving friend.

materials

- personal keepsake items: copy of photo, charms/buttons/shells, wire from champagne cork, afghan square
- place mat, ivory
- Lumiere metallic paint: Metallic Olive Green, Pearl Violet, Super Copper, Metallic Gold
- bubble wrap
- parchment paper
- iron
- velvet, dark blue, 11 x 14 in. (28 x 36cm)
- tulle, ivory
- sewing machine with lavender thread
- assorted fibers
- velvet, purple, 7 x 3 in. (18 x 7.6cm)
- ½ yd. (46cm) wide satin ribbon, rust
- ½ yd. fringe, sage green/ivory
- bamboo rod, 15 in. (38cm)
- fabric glue
- straight pins
- foam paintbrushes

1 Brush violet paint onto raised area of bubble wrap **[A]**. Press bubble wrap onto various areas of place mat. Repeat this step with remaining colors, creating a loose, random surface **[B]**. Let dry. Place parchment paper over painted place mat and press with medium-hot iron (no steam) for about a minute.

2 Lay velvet right side up on work surface. Cut random lengths of fibers and place them in a free-form pattern onto velvet. Allow yarns to dangle from top, sides, and bottom of velvet. Place several layers of tulle on top of yarns. Carefully pin all layers together **[C]**.

3 Take pinned layers to sewing machine. Sew layers together with medium-to-large zig-zag stitch. Keep stitched line curvy and loose on both front **[D]** and back **[E]**. Sew photo to lower right area of velvet.

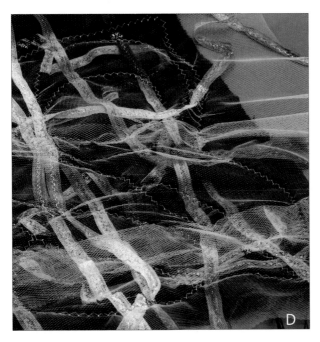

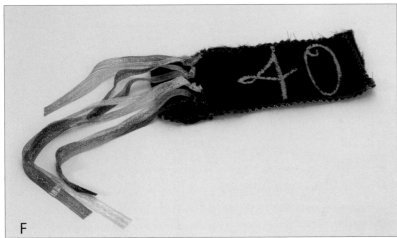

4 Sew assembled velvet piece onto place mat. Paint "40" onto right side of purple velvet rectangle using gold metallic paint. Let dry. Sew varying lengths of fibers to left edge of velvet. Sew around edges of velvet **[F]**. Glue assembled "40" velvet piece to left side of place mat.

5 Glue afghan square over upper left side of "40" velvet. Thread charms, buttons, and shells onto fibers dangling from "40" velvet. Glue additional charms, button, and champagne wire to lower right corner of photo.

6 Create a casing by stitching rust ribbon across top of place mat. Glue fringe trim below ribbon casing. Insert bamboo rod into casing. Tie three lengths of fibers to casing to form a hanger.

barb

Desk Treasures Retirement Remembrance

Look closely at ordinary office supplies, and interesting shapes and colors emerge. This piece is intended as a retirement keepsake, so make a point of asking the retiree for a few of her dusty desk-drawer remnants.

1 Working in a well-ventilated area, spray desk organizer with several coats of blue hyacinth paint. Allow paint to dry between coats.

2 Cut a piece of floral paper to fit within long section on left-hand side of desk organizer. Glue paper to bottom of section with fast-drying paper glue. Cut a few random flowers from remaining floral paper and glue to middle sections of desk organizer.

3 Use very light dabs of permanent glue to adhere five paper clips to upper area of left-hand organizer section. Use paper glue to adhere two colored pencils along right inside edge of section. Use permanent glue to adhere three paper clips inside bulldog clip. Adhere one small color pencil on top of bulldog clip. Glue assembled bulldog clip to bottom left, placing clip so that it crosses divider.

4 Use permanent glue to adhere ruler and rubber stamp to upper-middle organizer section. Paint photo corners orange and let dry. Apply a coat of gloss varnish and let dry. Insert photo into photo corners. Using paper glue, adhere assembled photo over part of yellow ruler.

5 Use very light dabs of permanent glue to adhere nine paper clips onto random sheets of old office memos or forms. Let dry completely. Cut paper around clips. Use fast-drying paper glue to adhere three groupings of assembled paper clips to second, fourth, and sixth small organizer sections on right-hand side. Use permanent glue to adhere three typewriter balls to remaining small organizer sections.

6 Use dimensional writer to draw outlines around glued paper flowers in middle organizer sections. Let dry completely.

7 Use permanent glue to adhere one large binder clip to center top of organizer tray. Adhere one small binder clip on either side of large clip.

materials

- desk-drawer organizer tray
- personal keepsake items: rubber stamp, old office memos or forms, 3 vintage typewriter balls, photo
- spray paint for plastic, blue hyacinth
- floral scrapbook paper
- old colored pencils
- 14 large plastic-coated paper clips, assorted colors
- large magnetic bulldog clip
- small plastic ruler
- 4 photo corners
- orange acrylic paint
- acrylic gloss varnish
- dimensional writer, white
- large binder clip
- 2 small binder clips
- fast-drying paper glue
- fine-tip permanent glue
- scissors
- paintbrush
- ruler

 TIP Display the finished keepsake on a simple plate stand or tabletop easel.

Nifty Fifty
Anniversary Art

L is the Roman numeral for 50. How nicely serendipitous that the word "love" begins with the letter *L*! A great big capital *L* is the focal point in this artwork that celebrates my parents' 50th wedding anniversary.

1 Use spatula or palette knife to spread a layer of molding paste onto canvas. This is like frosting a cake; as you spread the paste, create texture by forming peaks and valleys. Let dry thoroughly.

2 Paint canvas overall in sand color. Let dry.

3 Create a color wash by mixing three drops light mocha, four drops ochre, and three drops dark chocolate with about a tablespoon of water. Brush randomly over canvas, applying more color to edges of canvas. Let sit for a few minutes, then use rag to wipe and blot away random areas of color. Let dry.

4 Create a color wash by mixing five drops red, three drops maroon, and two drops dark chocolate with about a tablespoon of water. Brush randomly over canvas. Once again, apply more color to edges of canvas. Let sit for a few minutes, then use rag to wipe and blot away random areas of color. Let dry.

5 Paint wood *L* with several coats of red. Let dry. Mix black with a few drops of water and loosely paint around edges of *L*. Let sit a few minutes then wipe/blot with rag. Dry thoroughly. Mix equal parts red and water. Paint *L* overall, let dry a few minutes, then wipe/blot with rag. Let dry.

6 Use quick-gripping permanent glue to adhere *L* to left-hand side of canvas. Adhere photo corners to photos. Arrange photos to the right of the *L*. Use glue stick to adhere to canvas. Spell out "ove" with red marquee letters next to the capital *L*. Use tiny dots of quick-grip glue to adhere letters onto photos. Let dry.

TIP Molding paste is very light, easy to spread (like airy frosting!), and doesn't flake. Once dry, paste takes paint or delicate washes of color very nicely.

TIP This is a fun and simple project, but allow for a lot of drying time. Depending on where you live and the humidity factor, the air-dry clay can take up to 24 hours to dry fully.

7 Tear off a bit of air-dry clay and roll into a ¾-in. (1.9cm) ball. Press Celtic rubber stamp into ball of clay, flattening it out like a wax seal. Let clay dry thoroughly. Paint dried clay red. Let dry. Mix a tiny dot of black with several drops of water and brush onto clay. Let sit a few minutes then wipe/blot with rag. Let dry. Paint dried clay with satin varnish and let dry.

8 Wrap twine around canvas and tie into knot at front. Glue clay seal over knot, pressing down firmly. Let dry. Paint wooden frame black and let dry. Insert finished art into frame.

materials

- canvas panel, 14 x 11 in. (36 x 28cm)
- wood frame, 14½ x 11½ in. (36.8 x 29.2cm)
- personal photos
- light molding paste
- acrylic paint: sand, light mocha, ochre, dark chocolate, red, maroon, black
- satin varnish
- wood capital letter *L*, 9 in. (23cm)
- 8 photo corners, black
- marquee letters, red
- twine
- air-dry clay, red
- Celtic symbol rubber stamp
- glue stick
- quick-gripping permanent glue
- spatula or palette knife
- soft clean rag (a cotton T-shirt or sheet works well)
- large, soft paintbrush (a fan-shaped wash brush is ideal)
- scissors

Easter Basket Memories

Bring cherished Easter keepsakes together in a
fresh, contemporary frame. The result is a nostalgic
and meaningful piece of dimensional art just right
for a new grandbaby's nursery.

1 Open and separate EZ Snap frame into two pieces. Remove acrylic lens and spacer foam, and set aside.

2 Working in a well-ventilated area, spray larger (outer) frame with tanzanite spray paint. Use several coats to thoroughly cover frame. Allow paint to dry between coats. Repeat process, spraying smaller (inner) frame with yellow. Dry thoroughly.

3 Place acrylic lens and one foam spacer sheet into bottom of outer frame. Place green dotted cardstock on top. Use fast-drying paper glue to adhere cardstock to top of foam sheet.

4 Cut jute ribbon into two 12-in. (30cm) lengths. Repeat with checked ribbon. Use light dabs of fabric glue to adhere jute ribbon across top of dotted cardstock. Adhere checked ribbon directly below jute ribbon. Adhere remaining length of jute ribbon directly below checked ribbon.

5 Cut Easter card in half. Lay card halves on reserved foam spacer sheet. Trace around card shapes with felt-tip pen. Cut shapes from foam, cutting ¼ in. (6mm) inside traced lines. Use fast-drying paper glue to adhere card shapes to foam. Adhere assembled shapes to right and left bottom corners of dotted cardstock.

TIP Make handwritten notes about the items used in the piece: Who sent the sweet lamb card? How old were you when you received this Easter basket? Why did you save the goofy little chick? What was your favorite jellybean flavor? (Mine was licorice.) Sign the note and adhere it to the back of the frame so all those interesting thoughts and details are preserved.

6 Use fabric glue to adhere checked ribbon over card shapes, along bottom area of dotted cardstock. Cut 12 in. of rickrack and adhere above and slightly overlapping checked ribbon.

7 Use scissors and wire cutters as needed to cut bottom from old Easter basket. Adhere to center of cardstock area with fast-drying paper glue. Tie narrow pink ribbons around fuzzy chick's neck. Cut an 8-in. (20cm) length of rickrack and bundle with handful of basket grass. Bend chick's claws around center of bundle. Use fabric glue to adhere assembled chick onto center of Easter basket bottom.

8 Snap frames together. Use fabric glue to adhere rickrack across top and around to back of frame.

materials

- EZ Snap frame, white, 14 x 14 in. (36 x 36cm)
- spray paint: tanzanite, yellow
- cardstock, green dots
- 1 yd. (.9m) jute ribbon, sage green
- 1 yd. ribbon, pink/green check
- 2 yd. (1.8m) chenille rickrack, purple
- 12 in. (30cm) each narrow satin ribbon: pink, pink/white polka dot

- personal keepsake items: old Easter basket, handful of basket grass, fuzzy chick, Easter greeting card
- fast-drying paper glue
- fabric glue
- felt-tip pen
- wire cutters
- scissors
- ruler

Glitz & Glimmer Christmas Wreath

Mom's old costume jewelry and an outgrown wool sweater create a homespun wreath that will add sparkle and whimsy to your Christmas festivities.

A

materials

- craft foam wreath, 10 in. (25cm)
- personal keepsake items: costume jewelry pins, charms, bracelets, old wool sweater in Christmas pattern
- 2 yd. (1.8m) metallic bead trim, red
- pearl metallic corsage pins
- straight pins
- T-pins
- D-ring hanger
- foam glue
- fabric glue
- scissors

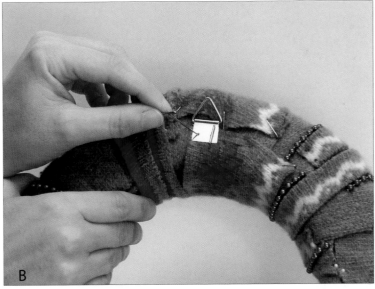

B

1 Machine-wash sweater in hot water and tumble-dry in hot dryer. This will shrink the sweater and turn it into a loose felt, which will prevent the wool from unraveling. Cut sweater into strips; cut some solid-color strips from sleeves and body, and some patterned strips from neckline and ribbing.

2 Wrap solid-color felt strips tightly around wreath form [A]. Dip tips of straight pins into foam glue and pin strips of felt into wreath as you wrap. Wrap and pin patterned strips of felt randomly around wreath, creating a pleasing pattern. Use large T-pins on back of wreath to secure thicker layers of felt into foam.

3 Wrap select areas of felt-covered wreath with red metallic bead trim. Adhere trim with small dabs of fabric glue. Let dry.

4 Position costume jewelry pieces around wreath to determine placement. (In this project, I chose to cluster my jewelry in three areas, creating a triangular formation, which is always pleasing to the eye.) Attach jewelry to wreath using corsage pins, dipping tips of pins into foam glue before pinning. Create a focal point in bottom-right area of wreath by gathering a long strand of red metallic bead trim and pinning it so that the ends dangle from wreath. Pin more jewelry over dangles.

5 Use large T-pins to attach a D-ring hanger to back of wreath [B].

Home for the Holidays Display Cube

Group some old holiday favorites and create a blast-from-the-past shadowbox to enjoy for many Christmases to come.

1 Spray shadowbox overall with several coats of red paint. Let dry between coats.

2 Tear a sheet of music to approximately 6 x 6 in. (15 x 15cm). Crush paper and smooth out. Mix gel medium and water to consistency of heavy cream. Brush back wall of box with gel medium. Adhere sheet music onto back wall, and brush with more gel medium to seal. Let dry.

3 Glue flat bottom of foam bell to lower right of back wall. Let dry. This will hold crocheted Santa ornament, which is a doorknob cover.

4 Use quick-gripping permanent glue to adhere small ornament to top left of box. Drill a small pilot hole in bottom center of box. Dip eye screw into a bit of glue, then screw into pilot hole. Hang vintage handmade ornament from eye screw. Glue elf figurine to top left of box. Let dry.

materials

- shadowbox, 6 x 6 x 3½ in. (15 x 15 x 8.9cm)
- personal keepsake items: family's hand-crafted Christmas ornaments, vintage elf figurine
- spray paint, red
- Christmas carol sheet music
- craft foam bell, 2½ in. (6.4cm)
- small eye screw
- matte gel medium
- foam glue
- quick-gripping permanent glue
- craft drill with ¹⁄₁₆-in. (2mm) bit

Retro Holiday Forest

Cones covered with graphic, vintage-style papers create this sleek and sparkly forest of Christmas trees. Childhood Christmas photos from the early '60s lend an additional feeling of nostalgia. Souvenir Mardi Gras beads become metallic tree garlands while adding a personal touch.

1 Spray several coats of glitter paint onto one sheet of blue cardstock. Let dry. Cut paper to fit top of foam block (you will need to piece it to cover). Use foam glue to adhere cardstock to block. Glue fur trim around outer edges of block. Use tacky glue to adhere light blue sequin trim around top edges of block.

2 Lay a medium-sized cone on a sheet of polka-dot paper, lining up bottom of cone with an edge of paper. Run several lines of foam glue along cone. Slowly roll paper around cone, using several straight pins to secure paper to cone. When cone is covered, carefully trim excess paper with scissors. (It's OK if the top and bottom of cone don't look great right now; these areas will be covered with trims and garlands later.) Repeat this process with remaining cones, using a variety of patterned papers.

3 Use tacky glue to adhere Mardi Gras beads and teal-and-white sequin trim around cones. Glue beads/trims around base of cones (this will hide any jagged paper edges left over from step 2).

4 Cut 4 in. (10cm) of silver garland and roll into a bundle. Apply a dab of tacky glue to center of bundle and pinch to secure. Apply glue around trimmed paper on top of small cone. Press bundle of garland into top of cone. Thread a corsage pin with a few metallic beads. Dip point of pin into foam glue. Press pin through center of garland and into top of cone. Repeat with medium cones. For large cones, follow the same steps, except add a wool felt bead to center of garland bundle before pushing corsage pin into cone.

5 Cut photos into 3-in. (7.6cm) circles. Glue one photo onto blue cardstock and the other onto orange cardstock. Trim cardstock, leaving a small mat around photo. Glue teal sequin trim around one photo and white trim around the other. Let dry. Turn assembled photos over and glue a strand of silver garland around back rim of each. Cut two 8-in. (20cm) lengths of teal sequin trim. Create loops with trim and glue one loop to back of each photo, creating a hanger. Hang a photo over each large cone, securing with corsage pins.

6 Use foam glue to adhere cones onto foam base created in step 1.

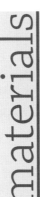

materials

- craft foam block, 6 x 14 in. (15 x 36cm)
- 2 craft foam cones, 9 in. (23cm)
- 2 craft foam cones, 6 in. (15cm)
- craft foam cone, 4 in. (10cm)
- personal keepsake items: photos, silver garland, Mardi Gras beads
- glitter spray paint
- 2 sheets cardstock, light blue, 12 x 12 in. (30 x 30cm)
- cardstock, light orange
- 2 yd. (1.8m) fake-fur trim, white
- sequin trims: light blue, teal, pearl white
- Christmas tree patterned paper
- polka-dot patterned papers
- straight pins
- pearl head corsage pins
- 12-14 metallic beads
- 2 wool felt beads: blue, green
- foam glue
- tacky glue
- scissors

HONOR

Heritage Stamp Collage

Postage stamps are a beautiful visual aspect of a country's culture. Combine stamps from your ancestors' country of origin with vintage photos to create a simple, elegant collage with historic flair.

Because I am of Irish and Polish heritage, I have purchased stamps from these countries over the years. Check your phone book for stamp store listings. Online Web sites are also good sources; the Polish stamps shown here came from polandbymail.com. Online auctions also are good sources.

1 Open and separate EZ Snap frame into two pieces. Remove acrylic lens and spacer foam, and set aside. (For the following steps, you may opt to wear latex gloves to protect fingers or manicures from alcohol ink stains. This can save you some cleanup time!) Apply a few drops denim-color ink to cosmetic sponge. Tap color onto outer plastic frame. Let dry. Apply a drop of espresso ink to another sponge and randomly tap over the denim color. Allow a bit of white frame to show through. Let dry.

2 Apply denim ink from sponge onto inner plastic frame. Dab and rub into corners and crevices with piece of felt. Let dry. Follow with espresso ink. Apply a few drops of blending solution to felt. Rub and blot solution randomly around inner frame. Blend and remove ink from some areas and leave other areas darker. (This process is all very loose and random. The results I like best always come from waiting for each color to dry before I apply the next color or solution.) Let frames dry thoroughly.

3 Glue textured tan paper to mat board. Tear maroon, sage, and blue cardstock and glue onto tan paper, allowing some tearing to show. Glue a 12-in. (30cm) length of black ribbon across top of layered papers. Tear photo around edges and glue to left-hand side.

4 Cut and tear gold and buff cardstock into long rectangular shapes and layer the buff onto the gold. Apply dimensional dots to the back and adhere assembled piece to lower right side of composition.

5 Glue six postage stamps to black cardstock and trim to create narrow black mat. Glue matted stamps to upper left area, and across buff/gold strip at bottom right. Glue two stamps to the upper right of photo.

6 Cut remaining black ribbon to 6 in. (15cm) and trim one end in a V-notch. Glue onto right side of composition, hanging down from one stamp. Typeset and print text of choice to fit within the metal oval frame. Cut text and glue into frame. Attach Claddagh charm to end of frame with jump ring. Glue assembled frame onto black ribbon.

7 Place assembled art into bottom of frame. Remove blue protective film from acrylic lens. Place acrylic lens over artwork. Place inner, top part of frame over art and snap frame pieces together.

materials

- EZ Snap frame, white, 14 x 14 in. (36 x 36cm)
- personal keepsake items: photocopy of grandparents' wedding photo on watercolor paper, silver Claddagh charm
- Adirondack alcohol-based ink: denim, espresso, blending solution
- Irish and Polish postage stamps
- mat board, 12 x 12 in. (30 x 30cm)
- textured scrapbook paper, tan
- cardstock: maroon, sage, blue, black, gold, buff
- self-adhesive dimensional dots, ⅛ in. (3mm)
- 1 yd. (.9m) grosgrain ribbon, black, 1½ in. (3.8cm) wide
- computer and printer
- small oval metal frame
- cosmetic sponges
- scrap piece of felt
- latex gloves (optional)
- silver jump ring
- jewelry pliers
- quick-dry paper glue

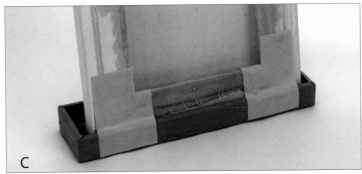

A

B

C

1 Spray front of c██████ ███y with spray adhesive.
Lay front of can████ ███ ██ satin. Trim satin around canvas, adding 5 in. ███ ██████ ████round. Wrap satin to back of canvas, mitering c██████ ██ ████educe bulk, and glue to canvas back with fabr██ █████ ███m any excess fabric.

2 Squeeze a generous ████ ██ of quick-gripping permanent glue into ████ ████back section of jewelry tray. Set canvas down into █████ ██. Prop front of canvas up with a full can of spray █ ████help canvas remain straight as glue dries **[B]**.

3 To stabilize canvas even fu████ ██ █ two lengths of wide scrap ribbon and glue █████ ██m back of canvas and down onto jewelry tray **[C]**.

4 Arrange chiffon scarf over top ██ █ canvas and secure with fabric glue. Drape ██████ █er left side of scarf over to side of canvas. Pinc██ █████ ██ue the gather onto side of canvas, allowing remain███ ████te of scarf to fall like a curtain. Slide a ring up fr██ ███ ██m of scarf and glue ring to scarf. Glue a large, da██ █████ring to scarf. Glue narrow black ribbon around ███ █████des of canvas.

5 Glue glove on a diagonal across front of canvas, leaving part of cuff loose. Fold cuff downward and glue a bracelet to cuff, tucking and gluing bracelet ends under glove. Glue three clip earrings to cuff.

6 Place photo of dress-up diva in frame. Use quick-grip glue to adhere assembled frame to canvas, over part of glove. Glue glove thumb to side of oval frame.

7 Squeeze quick-grip glue into jewelry tray at base of canvas. Place selected costume jewelry into glue, creating varying heights of jewels.

materials

- stretched canvas, 8 x 16 in. (20 x 41cm)
- personal keepsake items: photo, costume jewelry, formal gloves, chiffon scarves, jewelry box tray
- 1 yd. (.9m) acetate satin, pink
- wide scrap grosgrain ribbon
- 2 yd. (1.8m) narrow black satin picot-edge ribbon
- small black oval frame
- spray adhesive
- quick-gripping permanent glue
- fabric glue
- scissors

TIP The pink satin could be taken ██ little girl's outgrown ballet tutu██ princess costume, or security bl█

Cherished Voices Display Shelf

Over a period of years in the mid-'90s my sister Eileen interviewed our maternal grandparents, capturing all their fascinating and funny comments on eight cassette tapes. Eileen's voice is on the tapes as well, asking questions and reassuring our grandparents that they did, indeed, have something important to say. Since Grandma, Grandpa, and Eileen have all passed away, these tapes are especially meaningful. This little shelf is a unique way to visually display a very special audio collection. The papers collaged onto the background of the shelf are copies of family trees that Eileen also created. The photo is an old favorite of mine. (That's me on the left; wasn't I adorable?) Think about using the same treatment on your own genealogy-related items: a set of video tapes or a group of small photo albums that are a uniform size, for example, would work well.

materials

- bare wood shelf, 12 x 4 x 4 in. (30 x 10 x 10cm)
- personal keepsake items: genealogy photocopies, 10 copies of photo (with a large white margin all around), collection of cassette tapes
- acrylic paints: aqua, lemon
- matte gel medium
- solid wood whittler's kit
- metal quotation-mark brads
- quick-gripping permanent glue
- fast-drying paper glue
- bone folder
- ruler
- straightedge or triangle
- ruled cutting mat
- craft knife with new blade
- paintbrush
- red marker
- scissors
- wire cutters

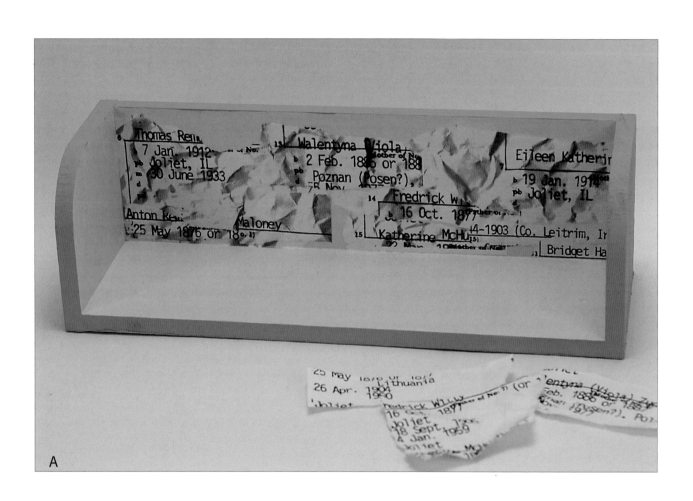

A

1 Paint shelf with 2-3 coats of lemon acrylic paint, allowing paint to dry between applications. Paint back, front, and side edges of shelf with 2-3 coats of aqua. Remove two 2 x 1 x ⅞-in. (5 x 2.5 x 2.2cm) wooden blocks and two 2 x 1½ x ⅞-in. (5 x 3.8 x 2.2cm) blocks from whittler's kit. Paint all blocks with 2-3 coats of aqua and set aside.

2 Tear genealogy photocopies into small pieces. Use paintbrush and matte medium to collage papers onto backrest of shelf **[A]**.

3 Enlarge or reduce your chosen photo so that it is slightly larger in size than the area of your lined-up cassette case spines. Make as many copies of your photo as you have cases to cover, plus 3-4 extras. Since I had

8 cassette cases to cover, I made 12 copies of my chosen photo so that I would have some to use just for measuring and a few extras just in case.

4 Lay a photo on your work surface. This photo will be your "spine guide" reference only. Using a red marker and ruler, divide photo into ⅝-in. (1.6cm) segments (the width of a cassette case spine), beginning at left edge **[B]**. This illustrates what part of the image will appear on each spine.

5 Lay a photo on your work surface. This will be the photo that wraps around your first, left-hand side cassette case. Using the case cover template (p. 75) and your spine guide reference, measure and mark photo to the size of a cassette case. Use a bone folder to score along the spine lines **[C]**.

B

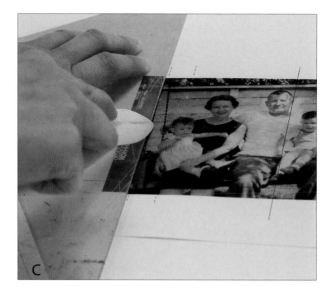

C

D

Score and fold on dotted lines

Cassette
case cover

4¼″
(10.8cm)

¾″
(1.9cm)

⅝″
(1.6cm)

2¾″
(7.0cm)

6 Use craft knife to carefully cut out photo; gently fold along scored lines. Wrap photo around first cassette case **[D]**. Glue in place with a few dabs of fast-drying paper glue. Repeat this process, moving along photo, until all cassette cases are covered. As you get closer to right-hand side, you may run out of excess photo paper to wrap around to front of case. Simply glue scrap strips of photos onto the case(s) to cover any plastic.

7 Line up finished cassette cases in center of painted shelf. Lightly mark left and right edges of grouping onto base of shelf. Create "bookends" by placing large painted blocks upright onto marked areas; use quick-gripping permanent glue to glue blocks to base of shelf. Glue small painted blocks next to large blocks. Let dry.

8 Use wire cutters to remove brad fasteners from metal quote marks. Use quick-grip glue to adhere quote marks to large upright painted blocks. Let dry. Place cassette grouping into place between quote marks.

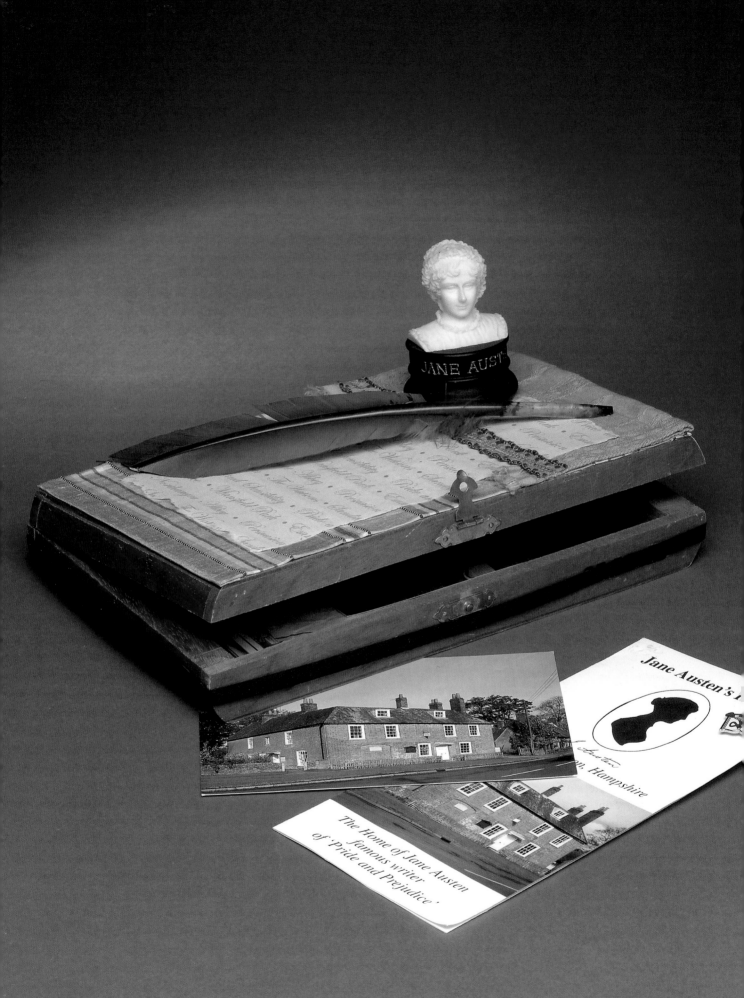

The Write Stuff Author Keepsake Box

Create a special keepsake box that pays tribute to a favorite author. This one features Jane Austen, one of my favorite writers. The box holds souvenirs from my visit to her home in Chawton, England.

1 Cut silk fabric to dimensions of box top, adding 1 in. (2.5cm) to width and height. With fabric glue, adhere silk to box top, turning edges under ½ in. (1.3cm). Cut gabardine to one-third the size of box top plus 1 in. on three sides. Glue to right-hand side of box top, turning three sides under ½ in. and leaving edge that shows on box top raw.

2 Using a computer word processing or graphics program, type list of author's works in typeface of choice. My type is set in a 5 x 7-in. (13 x 18cm) text block in 30-pt. Edwardian Script. Print in light blue ink onto ivory paper. Tear around text block. Use glue stick to adhere text to box top.

3 Glue ribbon approximately 3 in. (7.6cm) from right edge of box top. Trim any excess ribbon. Use quick-gripping permanent glue to adhere author bust to upper right edge of box top. Use small dabs of fabric glue to adhere feather quill to box top.

materials

- wooden cigar box
- personal keepsake items: Jane Austen bust, ink quill
- ½ yd. (46cm) pastel stripe silk
- ¼ yd. (23cm) textured sage green gabardine
- ¼ yd. ribbon, ½ in. (1.3cm) wide
- computer and printer
- ivory paper
- glue stick
- 1 yd. (.9m) bias tape, black, ¼ in. (6mm) wide
- fabric glue
- quick-gripping permanent glue
- ruler
- scissors or rotary cutter

TIP Use this concept to honor a favorite artist, dancer, or musician. If you can't find a bust of your favorite famous person, use a photo of her or him set inside a small frame or glued onto a cube. Embellish the frame to fit the person's style.

To the
memory of
Gandalf,
a fine mouser.
A solemn nap
will be
performed
in his
honor.
He will
be missed.

Kitty Keepsake Shrine

Our pets bring a special kind of love and enrichment to our lives, and their passing can leave us with a sharp sense of loss. An old collar and some catnip are incorporated into this charming shrine that celebrates the memory of a sorely missed kitty friend.

1 Cut two 8 x 10-in. (20 x 25cm) rectangles of green dotted paper. Use fast-drying paper glue to cover one piece of foam board with dotted paper. Wrap and glue paper around to back, mitering corners to reduce bulk. Trim excess paper and glue to cover any part of board that shows on back. Repeat with second foam board.

2 Glue pet photo to one paper-covered board. Tear purple paper to 2½ x 5½ in. (6.4 x 14cm). Glue paper to remaining board. Using computer, typeset and print out memorial sentiment for pet on white paper. Tear to about 1¾ x 5 in. (4.4 x 13cm). Adhere to purple paper. Add dots of red glitter paint to corners of white paper.

3 Cut three 1-in. (2.5cm) strips from pet's collar. Place covered boards next to each other (text on left; pet photo on right) with an ⅛-in. (3mm) gap between. Use fabric glue to adhere collar strips at three evenly spaced points, creating hinges that join the two boards. Let dry.

4 Paint matchbox cover and papier-mâché frame with two coats of turquoise paint, allowing paint to dry between applications. Remove bell from pet collar. Cut a small strip of green paper and loop it through the bell's ring. With quick-gripping permanent glue, adhere assembled piece onto one end of matchbox, creating a small drawer with pull. Let dry. Pour a thick layer of gel medium into matchbox drawer. Sprinkle generously with catnip, purple glitter, and gold micro beads. Let dry and shake out any loose bits after drying. Slide matchbox drawer halfway into matchbox cover. Glue assembled piece onto upper left-hand side of left board with quick-grip glue. Let dry. Add dots of red glitter paint to corners of matchbox cover.

5 Cut 18 in. (46cm) of fuzzy yarn and fold in half. Beginning with folded end, start to wrap around orange felt ball. Use dots of fabric glue to hold yarn in place as you wrap. Glue wrapped felt ball onto top of matchbox cover. Pull ends of yarn below matchbox, gluing as necessary, and make a coil near bottom of memorial text. Glue coil onto paper.

6 Brush edges of papier-mâché frame with gel medium. Sprinkle with catnip and purple glitter. Let dry. Apply dimensional dots to four corners of frame back. Position frame over selected area of pet photo. Use quick-drying paper glue to adhere frame to photo. Apply dots of red and gold glitter paint to frame.

7 Use fabric glue to adhere fuzzy yarn around pet photo. Knot ends of yarn near bottom left edge of photo and glue into place, allowing loose ends of yarn to dangle. Add a large dot of red glitter paint near knot.

materials

- 2 pieces foam board, each 4½ x 6½ in. (11.4 x 16.5cm)
- green paper with metallic dots
- purple handmade paper
- computer and printer
- personal keepsake items: pet photo, pet's collar with bell, catnip
- 2¼-in. (5.7cm) square papier-mâché frame
- matchbox (blanks available in craft stores, or recycle a used one)
- metallic acrylic paint, turquoise
- glitter paint: red, gold
- extra-fine purple glitter
- gold micro beads
- wool felt bead, orange
- 2 yd. (1.8m) fuzzy fashion yarn, purple
- dimensional dots
- matte gel medium
- quick-drying paper glue
- quick-gripping permanent glue
- ruler
- paintbrush
- scissors

Tribute to Eileen Collage

This collage on canvas is a very personal project in loving memory of my sweet sister, Eileen Maloney Szydlo. She was a librarian and loved writing and books, particularly the novels of Jane Austen. For this memorial tribute, I incorporated bits of paper printed with script, and a soft color palette reminiscent of England's Regency period.

materials

- heart-shaped tin, 3 in. (7.6cm) wide
- 2 mini "LOVE" tins, 2½ in. (6.4cm) wide
- white gesso
- canvas panel, 9 x 12 in. (23 x 30cm)
- iridescent transparent paints: turquoise, green, gold, red, violet, blue
- webbing spray paint: gold, white
- permanent marker, black
- toothpicks
- acrylic paint, sage green
- florist foam
- 2 glass vials, 1¾ in. (4.4cm)
- glass vial, 2¼ in. (5.7cm)
- glass spray paint: green, yellow
- oval "always" sticker

- decorative paper, 8½ x 11 in. (21.6 x 28cm)
- leaf bead
- 1 yd. (.9m) silk ribbon, mauve/sage, ½ in. (1.3cm) wide
- 1 yd. each metallic ribbon, ⅛ in. (3mm) wide: gold, pink
- 1 yd. metallic braid, peacock blue
- 1 yd. metallic facet braid, sky blue
- 2 heart-shaped ribbon buckles, copper
- 2 tassels, mauve
- permanent glue
- fabric glue
- dimensional glue dots
- paintbrush
- scissors

 TIP The heart-shaped tin is from a Valentine's Day mint promotion. Mini tins like the "LOVE" tins are often given as wedding favors; consider collaging your own using "LOVE" postage stamps.

1 Wash and dry tins. Brush gesso on inside and outside of heart-shaped tin and set aside to dry. Take lids off mini tins, reserving both. Use permanent glue to adhere bottoms of mini tins together. Press "always" sticker onto a long side of top tin.

2 Brush canvas panel with loose, diagonal strokes of turquoise iridescent paint thinned with a little water. Repeat with green paint, then gold. When dry, spray canvas with a light coat of white webbing spray **[A]**. Color a thin, loose border around canvas with black marker. Paint over black border with loose strokes of blue iridescent paint **[B]**.

3 Paint all gesso-primed areas of heart-shaped tin with sage green. When dry, brush same areas with violet iridescent paint. Let dry, then brush with two coats of red iridescent paint. Color rims of the open heart-shaped tin with black marker.

4 Push three short dowels or toothpicks into a piece of florist foam and invert a glass vial onto each rod. Spray glass vials with yellow paint, then green **[C]**. When dry, spray vials with light coats of gold and white webbing spray.

5 Tear a piece of decorative paper into a heart shape and glue onto painted underside lid of heart tin. Tear a piece of paper to approximately 2½ x 3½ in. (6.4 x 8.9cm) and fold into a fan shape. Insert into large glass vial and fan out the folds. Glue glass vial to inside bottom of heart tin. Glue a smaller vial on either side of large vial.

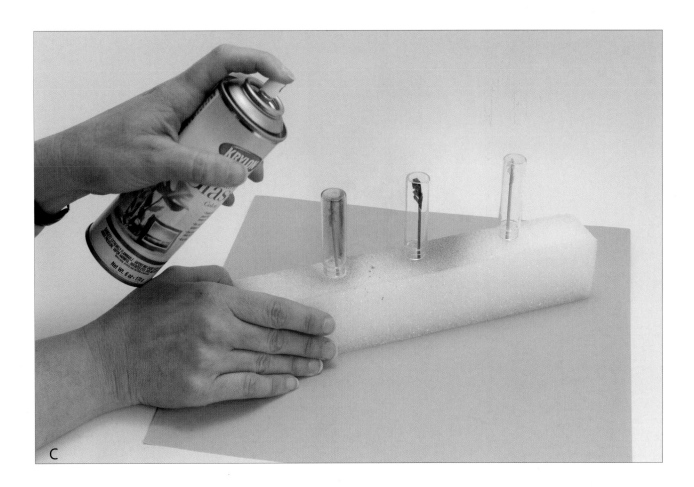

C

6 Paint inside raised panel of one mini tin lid with four coats of red iridescent paint. Color rim of lid with black marker. Paint over black marker with a coat of blue iridescent paint. When dry, use dimensional glue dots to adhere photo to inside of painted lid. Glue lid onto torn heart-shaped paper. Glue green leaf bead on top edge of photo lid.

7 Using permanent glue, arrange and adhere unpainted mini tin, assembled heart tin, and "always" tin vertically down center of canvas, as shown on p. 80.

8 Cut two 4½-in. (11.4cm) lengths of silk ribbon. Cut two each 4½-in. lengths of blue metallic facet braid and gold metallic ribbon. Thread one silk ribbon, one blue braid, and one gold ribbon through a heart-shaped ribbon buckle. Use fabric glue to adhere assembled piece to upper right corner of canvas, gluing excess ribbon around to back. Repeat for upper left corner of canvas.

9 Remove puffy slider from mauve tassels. Tie a knot 3 in. (7.6cm) above tassel. Cut excess cord close to knot. Glue knot just below heart-shaped ribbon buckle on upper right corner of canvas. Repeat for upper left corner.

10 Tear a strip of decorative paper to 11 x 1 in. (28 x 2.5cm) and glue horizontally across bottom of canvas. Turn excess to back and adhere. Cut silk ribbon to 11 in. and glue over script paper. Cut 18-in. (46cm) lengths from all metallic braids and ribbons, gather together, and tie a knot in the center. Tie additional knots approximately 3 in. to left and right of center knot. Glue knotted metallic ribbons on top of silk ribbon.

From
Marilu's
Garden

Flower Reflections

Pressed flower petals from a departed friend's garden are spotlighted in this piece of keepsake decor. The simple composition honors a woman who loved flowers, color, sparkle, and life.

1 Paint canvases with bright pink acrylic paint. Let dry. Stamp randomly with paisley design in brown ink. Let dry. Join canvases together by adhering brown satin ribbon down center front with fabric glue. Loop decorative ring through ribbon at top of canvas. Glue remaining brown ribbon down back sides of canvases and trim excess. Trim front ribbon into a V-notch.

2 Using computer, typeset and print desired sentiment to fit within silver tag frame. Cut out text and glue into frame. Attach flower brad to top loop of frame and open fasteners to secure brad. Glue assembled frame to top front of brown ribbon.

3 Cut photo into a circle to fit within glass tin lid. Glue photo below sentiment tag. Lightly dot permanent glue around rim of lid and adhere lid over photo. Glue pressed flower below photo, then glue lid over petal. Repeat process with remaining glass lids. Let dry.

4 Thread ribbon slide onto ivory satin ribbon. Using fabric glue, adhere ribbon across front and around to back of bottom canvas.

5 Adhere rhinestones to selected areas of stamped paisleys with tiny dots of permanent glue. Adhere one rhinestone to bottom center of framed sentiment. Adhere one rhinestone to center of ribbon slide.

materials

- 2 canvas panels, 5 x 7 in. (13 x 18cm)
- personal keepsake items: photo, pressed flowers
- acrylic paint, bright pink
- 1 yd. (.9m) satin ribbon, brown, 1½ in. (3.8cm) wide
- decorative ring, 1-in. (2.5cm) diam.
- 4 clear-glass tin lids
- ½ yd. (46cm) satin ribbon, ivory, ¼ in. (6mm) wide
- 7 rhinestones, pink
- paisley design rubber stamp
- permanent inkpad, brown
- computer and printer
- silver tag frame
- mini flower brad
- ribbon slide
- fine-tip permanent glue
- fabric glue
- paintbrush
- scissors

Dishes & Stitches Display

Grandma always prided herself on having a pretty (and scented!) handkerchief tucked into her pocketbook. She and my aunts worked their magic with embroidery and crochet to transform plain hankies, dresser scarves, and pillow shams into ladylike accessories. This grouping of various bits of the ladies' needlework, paired with some of their dainty glassware, is a fresh, sweet display honoring their efforts to add beauty and grace to everyday articles.

1 Trim crochet edging from the border of a dresser scarf. Glue around perimeter of cake stand.

2 Trim embroidered corners from three handkerchiefs or dresser scarves, creating triangle shapes. Glue corners to rims of glasses. Trim lace edgings from handkerchiefs and glue around rims of glasses, hiding any raw edges of handkerchief corners.

3 Arrange glasses on cake stand. Use a small pinch of putty on glass bottoms if desired. Place white votive candles or tea lights in glasses.

materials

- personal keepsake items: vintage embroidered handkerchiefs and dresser scarves
- 3-4 small glasses, various sizes
- glass cake stand, 9-in. (23cm) diam.
- fabric glue
- scissors
- putty adhesive such as Fun-Tak or museum putty (optional)

TIP Common sense precaution: Keep a close watch on candle flames, and don't leave candles burning unattended. Instead of candles, consider filling the glasses with fresh wildflowers. Or, in keeping with the needlework theme, fill with small "bouquets" of colorful crochet hooks or skeins of embroidery floss.

Grandpa's Workshop Remembrance

Honor the memory of a father or grandfather by arranging some of his well-used tools into a simple, meaningful composition. The focus on items that spent so much time in Grandpa's hands lends a sense of dignity to this art piece.

1 With glue stick, adhere photos to cardstock and trim, leaving area for handwriting, if desired. Punch random holes in cardstock. Arrange photos as desired on metal grate. Cut 15 in. (38cm) of wire and attach photos to grate, wrapping and twisting wire through punched holes and around grid lines of metal grate. Twist wire in back to secure, and trim excess.

2 Arrange tools as desired onto metal grate. Use dots of quick-gripping permanent glue to adhere tools to grate and secure firmly by wrapping tools to grate with wire. Twist and secure wire on back of grate and trim excess.

3 Break carpenter's rulers to create four 90-degree corner pieces. Break a few extra lengths of ruler. Sand rough edges. Use quick-grip glue to adhere a ruler to each corner of grate. Glue an extra length of ruler to upper left and lower right sides of grate. Let dry thoroughly.

4 Cut a leg from denim jeans and cut open at seam. Lay flat, right side up, on work surface. Place assembled grate over denim and cut around edges of grate. Place an old towel onto work surface and lay assembled grate face down on towel. Use fabric glue to adhere right side of denim to back of grate, pulling fabric as you glue to ensure a tight fit. Turn grate over. Trim excess denim from edges of grate. If denim is a bit loose in the center, use a pin or toothpick to apply dots

of fabric glue between metal and denim. Press down to ensure adhesion. Let dry.

5 To create a hanger, use a craft knife to poke some small holes on far right and left sides of the denim, about 3 in. (7.6cm) from top of grate. Thread a length of wire through holes and around to back of grate. Stretch wire across back of grate and twist wire to secure. Dot glue around holes in denim to ensure fabric will not rip.

materials

- personal keepsake items: old metal grate, tools, carpenter's rulers, photos, old denim jeans
- 22-gauge wire
- cardstock: rust, gold
- glue stick
- quick-gripping permanent glue
- fabric glue
- micro hole punch
- wire cutters
- medium-grit sandpaper
- scissors
- old towel

RESOURCES

Resources

Sometimes you may be inspired to track down the exact product I used in a project. With that in mind, here is a list of some of the specific products used, grouped by project. Please keep in mind that designs and products change. If you cannot find the exact item, you may be able to find a good substitute using these resource listings as a guide.

Millinery Memories, p. 24
Life's Journey round initial sticker *K&Company*

Toys & Treasures Collection Box, p. 26
Solid Wood Whittler's Kit *Walnut Hollow*
Just-Rite alphabet stamp *Millennium Marking Co.*

PB&J Artwork Display, p. 28
puffy heart trim *May Arts*

Coin of the Realm Shadowbox, p. 32
Classic Travel Poster Stickers *Dover Publications*

Travel Keepsake Tower, p. 34
Make It Suede textured spray paint *Krylon*
Expressions Rub-Ons, Journey *All My Memories*
Life's Journey Black Label Words & Sayings
K&Company

Old World Memory Map, p. 36
Texturizing Medium *DecoArt*

Joyful Season Card Display, p. 38
Mini-metallics Wax Rub-ons/Earthtones Kit #2
Craf-T Products
silver spiral clips *Creative Impressions*

Sweet Baby Keepsake, p. 42
baby-themed woven labels *Fun Expressions*

Happy Grad Keepsake Plate, p. 44
Perfect Paper Adhesive, Duo Embellishing Adhesive, Gildenglitz Variegated gilding leaf *USArtQuest*

Wedding Keepsake Decor, p. 46
JoLee's Woven Wedding Labels *EK Success*

Milestone Birthday Toast, p. 48
Moda Dea Spellbound Yarns: Majesty, Merlin, Wizard *Coats & Clark*

Desk Treasures Retirement Remembrance, p. 52
Fusion spray paint for plastic *Krylon*
Mia's Collection floral scrapbook paper *Adornit*
Americana white dimensional writer *DecoArt*

Nifty Fifty Anniversary Art, p. 54
light molding paste *Golden*
Spare Parts red marquee letters *Stampabilities*
air-dry clay *Makin's Clay*
Celtic symbol rubber stamp *Hero Arts*

Home for the Holidays Display Cube, p. 60
Christmas carol sheet music *Dover Publications*

Retro Holiday Forest, p. 62
glitter spray paint *Krylon*
Christmas Tree Parade paper *Paper Fever*
Be-Bop polka dot papers *s.e.i.*
wool felt beads *Artgirlz*

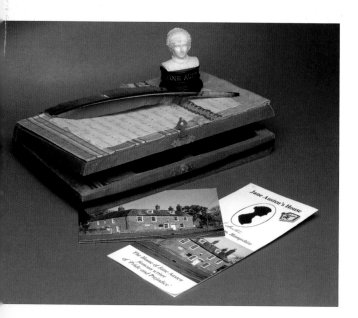

Resources

Look for the specific products listed in this book at art, craft, rubber stamp, scrapbooking, and specialty stores. The manufacturers listed here can direct you to a retail source for their products.

AdornIt
Carolee's Creations
papers
(435) 563-1100
adornit.com

Around The Block
brads, embellishments
(801) 593-1946
aroundtheblockproducts.com

Artgirlz
charms, felt flowers, beads
(401) 244-5819
artgirlz.com

Avery
iron-on transfer paper
(800) 462-8379
avery.com

Beacon Adhesives
Fabri-Tac, Gem-Tac, Quick Grip,
3-in-1 Craft Glue
(914) 699-3405
beaconcreates.com

Blue Moon Beads
beads, charms, jewelry findings
(800) 377-6715
bluemoonbeads.com

Cheeptrims
trim
(877) 289-8746
cheeptrims.com

Clearsnap
pigment and dye inks
(800) 448-4862
clearsnap.com

Coats & Clark
fashion yarns
(800) 648-1479
coatsandclark.com

Craf-T Products
wax rub-ons
craf-tproducts.com

Creative Impressions
embellishments
(719) 596-4860
creativeimpressions.com

DarStar Enterprises
frames
(630) 243-8600
darstarent.com
*EZ Snap frames from DarStar
Enterprises have acrylic panes that
help protect your finished work
from UV rays.*

DecoArt
paint
decoart.com

Dover Publications
clip art
doverpublications.com

EK Success
embellishments
eksuccess.com

Fun Expressions
embellishments
(800) 875-8480
orientaltrading.com

Golden Artist Colors, Inc.
gel medium, paint
(800) 959-6543
goldenpaints.com

**Graphic Products
Corporation**
skeleton leaves
(800) 323-1660
gpcpapers.com

Hero Arts
rubber stamps
(800) 822-4376
heroarts.com

Jacquard Products
paint
(800) 442-0455
jacquardproducts.com

**Jo Sonja's Iridescent
Acrylics**
Chroma, Inc.
paint
(717) 626-8866
chromaonline.com

K&Company
embellishments
(888) 244-2083
kandcompany.com

Kreinik Mfg. Co., Inc.
metallic fibers
(800) 537-2166
kreinik.com

Krylon
spray paints and adhesives
(800) 457-9566
krylon.com

Lavender Lane
glass vials
(541) 474-3551
lavenderlane.com

Making Memories
embellishments
(801) 294-0430
makingmemories.com

Makin's Clay
air-dry clay
(402) 891-0085
makinsclay.com

May Arts
ribbon
mayarts.com

Millennium Marking Co.
JustRite Stampers adjustable
type rubber stamps
justritestampers.com

Mokuba
ribbon
(212) 869-8900
mokubany.com

Nunn Design
metal embellishments
(800) 761-3557
nunndesign.com

Provo Craft
papier mâché letters
(800) 937-7686
provocraft.com

Ranger Industries, Inc.
inkpads
(732) 389-3535
rangerink.com

Rings & Things
beads, charms
(800) 366-2156
rings-things.com

s.e.i.
paper
(800) 333-3279
shopsei.com

SKS Bottle & Packaging, Inc.
metal tins
(518) 880-6980
sks-bottle.com

Stampabilities
rubber stamps,
embellishments
(800) 888-0321
stampabilities.com

The Dow Chemical Co.
Styrofoam brand craft foam
craft.dow.com

USArtQuest
gold-leafing supplies, glue
(800) 766-0728
usartquest.com

Walnut Hollow
wooden boxes, shelves,
whittler's kits
(800) 950-5101
walnuthollow.com

Mary Lynn Maloney is a mixed-media artist and author with a background in graphic design and a degree in arts and humanities. She grew up in a large Irish-Polish family where the arts, reading, creativity, and imagination were highly encouraged. Mary Lynn's elegant, thoughtful, and unconventional designs are regularly featured in crafting magazines and books. In addition to her design work, Mary Lynn creates found-object assemblage art and collage that she exhibits in a local gallery. She lives in Port Townsend, Wash., with her husband, Victor Judd; their two cats, Simba and Loki; and 37 trees, which they haven't named yet.

A little about the art car

When my 13-year-old Miata started to look a little worn and tired, I decided against repainting her in the conventional way. I wanted an art car, like those I'd seen over the years at festivals and parades. I lived in Dallas at the time, where the automobile as status symbol reigns supreme. I thought it would be fun to create something that was whimsically opposite to this notion. A group of talented and artistic friends helped me create the MiArta using paint, glue, beads, coins, and assorted tchotchkes. I asked only that they include their handprint, fingerprint, or footprint somewhere in their little section of the car. The results were glorious. The car is a little rolling piece of memory art for me that includes the collective creative energy of friends and family.

– Mary Lynn

THANK YOU

As always, special thanks to my parents, Jim and Shirley Maloney, for all their support. Sincere thanks to the manufacturers who provided materials for many of the projects. Thanks so much to Adria Ellis, Mary Mueth, Barbara Durham, and Amy Baker for their help with photographs, and to Victor for the step-by-step and author photos. Big thanks and hugs to my nieces, nephews, and grandkids for providing me with a delightful collection of artwork to display. Thanks to Pat Durbin for the elegant opera glasses. And many thanks to my super-sharp editors, Pat Lantier and Mary Wohlgemuth, for their encouragement, enthusiasm, and helpful perspective.